INDIANS

OF THE NORTHWEST

Edited by Rochelle Cashdan

Tlingit Baskets, with geometric patterns, except the lower left basket, which is designed with a killer whale motif (Courtesy of the American Museum of Natural History)

Discovery Enterprises, Ltd.
Carlisle, Massachusetts

All rights reserved. No part of this book may be reproduced, stored in a retrieval system, or transmitted in any form or by any means, electronic, mechanical, photocopied, recorded, or otherwise, without prior written permission of the authors or publisher, except for brief quotes and illustrations used for review purposes.

© Discovery Enterprises, Ltd., Carlisle, MA 1998

ISBN 1-57960-014-X paperback edition
Library of Congress Catalog Card Number 97-77591

10   9   8   7 6   5   4   3   2   1

Printed in the United States of America

Subject Reference Guide:

Indians of the Northwest
edited by Rochelle Cashdan
Indians/Native Americans — U.S. History
Northwest Indians — U.S. History

Photos/Illustrations Credits:

Photos and illustrations were selected by the Publisher.

Front cover: Fisherman in his canoe on the
Columbia River, The Dalles Oregon, 1897.

Illustrations on pages 6, 53, and both front and back covers
are from *The Lost Field Notes of Franklin R. Johnston's Life and
Work Among the American Indians,* First Glance Books, Inc.,
Cobb, CA: 1997. (707-928-1994)

All other photos and illustrations are credited where they appear in book.

Table of Contents

Foreword

by Rochelle Cashdan

As I was putting together this collection of readings, I started thinking of the Indians of the Northwest as "the persisting peoples." Like the many peoples called "Europeans," Northwest Indian groups have much in common and much that is different from group to group.

In the Northwest, people have lived near river mouths and ocean beaches for thousands of years; other homelands were the long, grassy inland valley along the Willamette River; the great Columbia and other inland rivers, upland lakes, and the semi-desert.

West of the Cascade Mountains, people heard rain falling on the roof during the cooler half of the year. Then would come the dry season beginning in mid-spring and continuing until fall. East of the mountains, most people had a four-season climate, with cold winters and hot dry summers. Winter could also be cold and cruel in the Columbia Gorge.

Indian families and bands were not alone in this land. Depending where they lived, there were salmon, deer, rabbits, tall trees, brush, reeds, bulbs, roots, and berries, all useful to humans. The people lived in villages or camps, with many groups having both winter and summer locations. Each group had its own language or dialect, with many people speaking more than one language. Each put its own stamp on its culture, identity, worldview, and ways of organizing its society. But, whether they hunted whales or rabbits, the people had certain ways in common. Storytelling is one.

Into this long-existing way of life, came the Euroamericans — at first in a trickle, later in great numbers. At first, came the Spanish and farther north the Russians; then French and English traders; and then, in the 1830s, a growing stream of settlers and missionaries. With smaller numbers and less power behind them, the Indian peoples could no longer control the use of the land by the mid-19th century. They had to accept the rule of others.

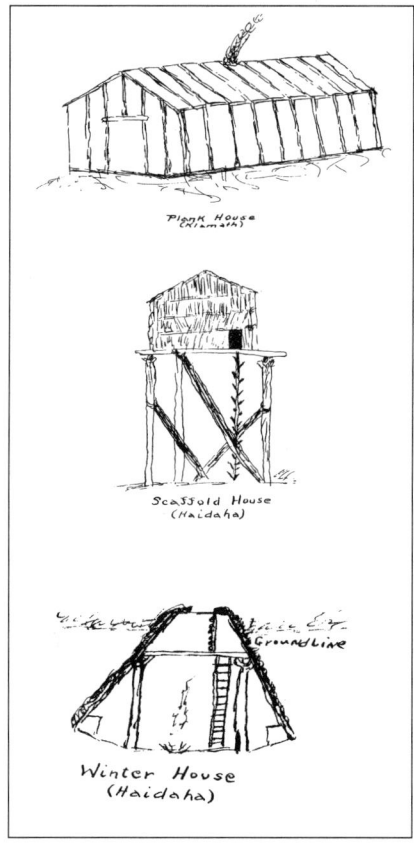

Franklin R. Johnston's sketches of Northwest Indians' types of dwellings.

But through all the diseases, wars, intermarriage and political difficulties, Indian identity persisted. Sometimes, a few people kept the heritage alive for a whole group; other more fortunate groups remained more intact.

Like other people, all Indians even in one tribe, do not choose the same lifestyle. Some are learning the old languages or serving in the U.S. military or speaking for their tribes. Some dance at pow-wows, create new stories, poems, and art. Some travel as far as Austria or Ceylon, where people far from our shores take an interest in their lives and issues.

Editor's Note: This sourcebook focuses mainly on tribes now based in Northern California, Oregon, Washington, Idaho, and Alaska. I regret not having space to mention all the tribes in this small book. If you are interested in the tribes in Canada, several books listed as Suggested Further Reading can give you some suggestions. The list is just a starting point. Hundreds of books about Indians exist — including an increasing number prepared by Indian writers and editors — and there are many tribal cultural centers and museums where a person can learn.

Introducing Yourself in the Indian World

Introductory note from a recent guidebook prepared in cooperation with the Affiliated Tribes of the Northwest.

Source: Jan Halliday and Gail Chehak, *Native Peoples of the Northwest*, Seattle: Sasquatch Books, 1997, p. 6.

When greeting each other, Native people rarely use the words "Indian," "Native," "Native American," or "First Nation." Instead they describe themselves according to their tribal affiliation and ancestry. Someone who is an enrolled member of the Spokane Nation in Washington State might say, "I'm Spokane, with Coeur d'Alene and Welsh. My mother is Spokane, my father is Coeur d'Alene, and my grandfather is Welsh."

When you meet a Native person, just identify yourself as you would to anyone else. If you want to discuss heritage with a Native person, be prepared to know your own. For example, Jan Halliday might say "My family were lowland Scots who moved to Washington in the 1800s. What Jan is saying is that she descends from a long line of settlers. When Gail Chehak says, "I'm Klamath," she is saying that she descends from people who have lived for more than 500 generations on marshland in present-day southeastern Oregon. Encoded in both of these short introductions is a wealth of history and legend. What really matters, though, is the respect that Gail and Jan have for each other, and for each other's family history.

Accounts of Traditional Lifeways

The spirit of a people comes in part from its account of how the world began. For Indian people, that spirit also comes from passing on stories of combined animal-human beings from a time before human society. The teller often uses humor, making the stories all the more memorable to each generation hearing them for the first time.

Much of the knowledge of old values and skills handed down is not in books. People learn as they grow up and pass along what they know to their children. Particular activities change: travel now depends on cars, planes, and buses, not canoes or horses, but values like practicality, participating in Indian gatherings, skill in negotiating, and the importance of grandparents persist.

Meninock's Story of Creation

Among Indians, stories are told at the time that seems right, the appropriate season or when the teller wants the lesson of the story to come through. Here is a twentieth century transcript of a Yakima headman's words. He is explaining his people's view of creation to the federal judge hearing a case about the Yakima people's treaty rights to fish. (Yakama-the new official spelling of Yakima.) (Also see page 23.)

Source: Wayne Moquin, ed., *Great Documents in American Indian History*, New York: Praeger, 1973, pp. 297-298. Testimony from a U.S. Court case, 1928, from the *Washington Historical Quarterly*, July 1928, pp. 17-174.

God created this Indian country and it was like He spread out a big blanket. He put the Indians on it. They were created here in this country, truly and honestly, and that was the time this river started to run. Then God created fish in this river and put deer in these mountains and made laws through which has come the increase of fish and game. Then the creator gave us Indians life; we awakened and as soon as we saw the game and fish we knew that they were made for us. For the women God made roots and berries to gather, and the Indians grew and multiplied as a people. When we were created we were given our ground to live on, and from that time these were our rights. This is all true....It matters not how long I live, I cannot change these thoughts.

Kalapuya Myth...when animals were people

Scholar Dell Hymes translated this long myth told by William Hartless (Kalapuya) in Kalapuya in 1914 to another anthropologist. The beginning that you read here about a child's death is about a one-sixth of the full story. The translator has divided the story into short lines that show the phrasing passed down by one storyteller after another. During the mythtime in this story, animals had the thoughts and emotions of people.

Source: Brian Swann, ed., "Coyote, Master of Death, True to Life," found in *Coming to Light, Contemporary Translations of the Native Literatures of North America*, New York: Random House, pp. 286-306.

....

Now then Panther's daughter fell ill,
   she died.
Now then Panther said,
   "I will go see my brother."
Now then he said to his brother, Coyote,
   "How is your heart about it?
   When a person dies,
   The fifth day he will come back?"
Coyote said nothing.

10

Again indeed he said to his brother,

    "How is that thing I told you?"

Coyote said,

    "No, it must not be that way.

    If it were to be that way where people live,

      the number of people would be endless.

    Better that a person die for all time.

For all time he will be gone."

Panther said,

    "Ohh no! Brother!

    Better really that they come back."

Coyote said,

    "Not now!

    Everything that is,

      the black water bugs themselves would say,

        'Where are we to stay?' "

Coyote said,

    "Let it be that way when a person dies.

    That way he will indeed die for all time."

Panther said,

    "Your own heart."

Now then Panther went back.

    He wept.

  He buried his daughter.

Now then one year later Coyote's daughter fell ill,

    she died.

    Now then Coyote said,

    "Well now brother!

Let it be the way you told me."

Panther said,

  "It cannot be that way now."

Coyote said,

  "Ohh it would be better that people come back,

    on the fifth day they awaken."

Panther said,

  "Not now!

  You already said,

    'When a person dies he is to be dead indeed for all time.'

  You spoke that way,"

    Panther said.

Now then Coyote went back,

  he wept and wept,

   he got back home,

    he said,

     "I will go myself.

  He said to his daughter,

    "I will go myself.

    We will go together."

  His daughter said,

    "you can't follow me now.

    It is another kind of country where I am going."

  Coyote said,

    "It's no matter that I go myself."

  Now then he made a rope....

Quileute Account of Canoe-making

In 1928, scholar Roy de Andrade wrote down Jack Ward's comparison of old and new ways of canoe-making. Ward was talking in the Quileute language.

Source: Manuel Jose Andrade, ed., *Quileute Texts*, New York: Columbia University Press, 1931, p. 2.

First one goes up the river toward the swamps to look for a good tree to make the tail, the river canoe, out of. When he finds a good tree, he goes back home to look for the ones who are going to help him. They go back to the tree and cut it down. After felling a tree that can serve such a purpose, they don't dare come near it, because the power of the tree would make them sick. There is no doubt that it would, because the expert canoe-maker knows it, and one does not usually become a canoe-maker without spirit help. Nowadays it is different, because we have acquired White people's tools.

Chief Mark on Monogamy

Chief Mark at Warm Springs makes a statement to Agency Superintendent A.P. Meacham about the Superintendent's proposed policy substituting non-Indian marriage customs for the marriage customs of his tribe. Meacham, whose policies were not always welcomed by Indians, had his clerk keep careful records of statements like Mark's.

After hearing the statement, Meacham ruled that the new policy would only apply to new marriages and not to marriages like Chief Mark's made in the past.

Source: Alfred B. Meacham, *Wigwam and Warpath*, Boston: Rockwell & Churchill, 1876, pp. 174-175.

My heart is warm like fire, but there are cold spots in it. I don't know how to talk. I want to be a white man. My father did not tell me it was wrong to have so many wives. I love all my women. My old wife is a mother to the others, I can't do without her; but she is old, she cannot work very much; I can't send her away to die.

This woman cost me ten horses; she is a good woman; I can't do without her.

That woman cost me eight horses; she is young; she will take care of me when I am old.

I don't know how to do; I want to do right. I am not a bad man. I know your new law is good; the old law is bad. We must be like the white man. I am a man; I will put away the old law....I want you to tell me how to do right. I love my women and children, I can't send any of them away; what must I do?

Teaching Children to Behave

At an intertribal Indian Education Conference, educator Alex Saluskin (Yakama) recalls the ways adults in his village used to oversee the behavior of the children when he was growing up. He is talking about a time when he and his friends had been hard on a horse that died a short time later.

Source: Wayne Moquin, ed., *Great Documents in American Indian History*, New York: Praeger, 1973, p. 298. (Testimony from a U.S. Court case, 1928.)

After construction of the long houses of a new village there was a ceremony to whip these little fellows that had been mischievous for a certain period of time. Each family came and had a report. How many children were involved in this mischief? And we have to say we were. How about this other mischief that was committed? A lot of them were in that too. No one denied it, because they were asked. They were taught honesty. The result was that a hired whipper delivered the punishment. He lined you up, tied the willow rods together, about seven. He let you kneel down in front of all the families, relatives and old folks. That fellow brings his whip up and

14

right across your back just as hard as he could. By about the third blow, you don't feel anything. That was what they give you — three. Some of those smart ones think, "If I turn over and start to whimper, they'll take pity on me and won't whip me." That was worse on them, as that whip man was going to let that punishment come down. All received the same, even the one that was good enough to report us.

The philosophy of that was if you're playing and somebody commences to suggest some mischief, you know somebody is going to tell, and we'll get a licking. Let's not do it.

A Klamath Man Remembers Learning to Hunt

In the 1950s, an older member of the Klamath tribe whose first language was Klamath and second language English tells a graduate student in anthropology how he learned to hunt.

Source: Hiroto Zakoji, *Klamath Culture Change*, Master's thesis, Department of Anthropology, University of Oregon, 1953, p. 241.

T. L. (Klamath): First time, I started to hunt ducks first. I loaded a shot gun and there was lots of ducks. I was afraid to touch the trigger. I put it on the fence and tried to pull the trigger with a stick. Someway, I had to put it down. I was afraid. Finally, I took another gun. I was afraid to shoot but someway I touch the trigger and killed a rabbit. Then I wasn't afraid so I took the shotgun again. I became a good hunter. I learned by myself by watching other people. Nobody taught me. I learned by watching. I didn't tell my grandpa about that shotgun because he might think I am poor hunter. After I killed the rabbit I brought it into camp and my grandmother cooked it with bacon. My grandpa was pretty proud and told everyone, "Here comes hunter with game." Everyone was proud of me. After that, I came home with rabbit every day almost. Rabbits in fall is good and fat.

Outsiders Come into the Indian Lands

Spaniards and then Russians, French and English traders and missionaries came to the Northwest region before the famed overland expedition of Lewis and Clark. The expedition signaled the impending arrival of large numbers of people who wanted to settle and own land. Their concept of exclusive ownership, rather than rights to use, led to friction concerning the two ways of life.

President Thomas Jefferson interested himself in the details of the expedition into Indian lands where Meriwether Lewis, William Clark, and the members of the expedition would be going with Sacajawea (Shoshone) as their guide and interpreter. Jefferson's instructions showed the President's attitudes toward expanding commercial opportunities and "instructing and civilizing" native peoples. (Several key passages from this letter can be found in Westward Expansion: Exploration and Settlement, *Cheryl Edwards, ed., pp. 13-17. Perspectives on History Series, Discovery Enterprises, Ltd., Lowell, MA: 1995.)*

Supply List for Lewis and Clark's Trading with the Indians

Supplies for the expedition and anticipated gifts for trade with the Indians were an important element in planning the trip. The supplier kept careful accounts of purchases, with about a third of the expenditures allotted for "gifts" to the Indians. Most of these items were for practical purposes or decorative use. Note that a dollar in 1802 would buy about as much as $30 now.

Source: Donald D. Jackson, ed., *Letters of the Lewis and Clark Expedition, with related documents, 1783-1854*, Urbana: University of Illinois Press, 1962, pp. 93-94.

Recapitulation of Purchases by The Purveyor for Capt. Lewis

Mathematical Instruments	412.95
Arms, Ammunition & Accoutrements	182.08
Medicines &c.	94.49
Clothing	317.73
Provisions &c.	366.70
Indian Presents (see below)	669.50
Camp Equipage	116.68
[Total $]	2160.14

Indian Presents

12 Pipe Tomahawks

6 1/2 lbs. Strips Sheet Iron

1 Ps. red flannel 47 1/2 yards

11 Ps. hanckerchiefs assd.

3 doz. Ivory Combs

1/2 Catty India. S. Silk

21 lbs. Tread assd.

1 Ps. Scarlet Cloth 22 yds. about 550

5 1/2 doz. fancy 1 Floss

6 Gro. Binding

2 Cards beads

4 doz. Butcher Knives

12 doz. Pocket Looking Glasses

15 doz. Pewter do.do.

8 doz. Burning do.

2 doz. Nonesopretty

2 doz. Red strip'd tapes

72 ps. Strip'd silk ribbon

3 lbs Beads

6 Papers Small Bells

1 box with 100 larger do.

73 Bunches Beads assd.

3 1/2 doz.: Tinsel Bands assd.

1 doz: needle Cases

2 3/4 doz. Lockets

8 1/2 lbs. Red Beads

2 doz. Earings

8 brass Kettles a 4/lb

12 lbs. Brass Strips

500 Broaches

72 Rings

2 Corn Mills

15 doz. Scissors

12 lbs. Brass Wire

14 lbs. Knitting Pins

4600 Needles assd.

2800 Fish Hooks assd.

1 Gro. Iron Combs

1 Gro. Curtain Rings

2 Gro. Thimbles assd.

11 doz. Knives

10 lbs. Brads

8 lbs. Red lead

2 lbs. Vermillion 130 Rolls of Tobacco (pigtail)

48 Callico Ruffled Shirts

15 Blankets (from P. Store)

1 trunk to pack sundry Ind. Prests.

8 Groce Seat or Mockasin Awls.

[Total cost] $669.50

From the Journals of Lewis and Clark

As instructed, Meriwether Lewis and William Clark kept copious notes on their travels, notes which are highly readable today despite their spelling and punctuation. The October 22 entry describes their arrival at Celilo Falls after passing many falls and villages on the Columbia River and document the techniques used by the women to preserve the fish caught by the men. They stored the pounded product in baskets and mats. There is evidence of a salmon economy along the Columbia and its tributaries as long as 9000 years ago.

Source: Bernard DeVoto, ed., *The Journals of Lewis and Clark*, Boston: Houghton Mifflin, 1953, pp. 246, 261-262.

October 10, 1805 Thursday [Clark]

Our diet extremely bad haveing nothing but roots and dried fish to eate, all the Party have greatly the advantage of me, in as much as they all relish the flesh of dogs, Several of which we purchased of the natives for to add to our store of fish and roots &c, —

The Chopunnish or Pierced nose Indians are Stout likely men, handsom women and verry dressey in their way, the dress of the men are a White Burralow robe or Elk Skin dressed with Beeds which are generally white, Sea Shells & the Mother of Pirl hung to the[i]r hair & on a piece of otter skin about their necks hair Ceewed in two parsels hanging forward over their Sholders, feathers, and different Coloured Paints which they find in their Countrey Generally white, Green & light Blue....

Captains Lewis & Clark holding a Counal with the Indians

Patrick Gass published this etching in his account of the expedition in 1811. Gass was a member of the Corps of Discovery.

October 22d Tuesday 1805 [Clark].

About half a mile lower passsed 6 more Lodges on the Same Side and 6 miles below the upper mouth of Towornehiooks [Des Chutes] River the commencement of the pitch of the great [Celilo] falls, opposit on the Stard. Side is 17 Lodges of the nativs we landed and walked down accompanied by an old ma to view the falls and the best rout for to make a portage....

Indians assisted us over the portage with or heavy articles on their horses, the waters is divided into Several narrow channels which pass through a hard black rock forming Islands of rocks at this stage of the water, on those Islands of rocks as well as at and about their Lodges I observe great numbers of Stacks of pounded Salmon neetly preserved in the following manner, i.e. after [being] suffi[ci]iently dried it is pounded between two Stones fine, and put into a spces of basket neetly made of grass and rushes better than two feet long and one foot Diamiter, which basket is lined with the

Skin of Salmon Stretched and dried for the purpose, in this it is pressed down as hard as is possible, when full they Secure the open part with the fish Skins across which they fasten th[r]o. the loops of the basket that part very securely, and then on a Dry situation they Set those baskets the corded part up, their common custome is to Set 7 as close as they can Stand and 5 on the top of them, and secure them with mats which is raped around them and made fast with cords and covered also with mats, those 12 baskets of from 90 to 100lbs. each form a Stack. thus preserved those fish may be kept Sound and sweet Several years, as those people inform me, Great quantities as they inform us are sold to the whites people who visit the mouth of this river as well as to the nativs below.

Treaties and Troubles

Ed Meninock Recalls Treaty Council, 1855

As a boy, Ed Meninock accompanied his father to the momentous council at Walla Walla in 1855. Seventy-three years later, he carried on the family tradition of representation, this time at a federal court, over maintaining treaty rights to fish, an issue which would continue coming up time and time again.

Source: In Wayne Moquin, ed., *Great Documents in American Indian History*, New York: Praeger, 1973, p. 298. Testimony from a U.S. Court case, 1928.

I was at the Council at Walla Walla with my father, who was one of the chiefs who signed that treaty. His name was Meninock, too. Jim Wallahee, who was arrested when I was and who is a defendant too, had an uncle whose name was Owhi, who was at that council and who also signed the treaty. I well remember hearing the talk about the treaty. There were more Indians there at Walla Walla than ever came together any place in this country. Besides the women and the children, there were two thousand Indian warriors, and they were there for about one moon, during the same part of the year as now, in May and June....

Our chiefs did not want to sign the treaty proposed by General Stevens. Our father [Chief Kamiaken] said, 'You will take away our rights and we cannot fish and hunt,' and they would not sign the treaty. There was much trouble then.

General Stevens said: 'You listen to me. I am going to protect you in your rights to fish. I will put in the record never to be wiped out that the Indians shall have the right to fish at their fishing places. I will see that your children get their rights. If, when I am gone, any of my white children violate this agreement the government will punish them — the government will take up and protect you always as long as the sun shines, as long as the mountains stand and as long as the rivers run.'

Then our chiefs were persuaded and they believed what General Stevens said and they signed the treaty and the clouds cleared away and the day was bright.

....

No people can fight against the Americans. Only the great God himself can punish them when they do wrong. I am now old; you are powerful; you can wipe away our tears, order your officers to be just; forbid them to arrest the Indians when they fish at places reserved in the treaty; have pity on us. You have many red children here; grant them their rights.

Articles from the Treaty with the Quinaielt

1855 was a key year for treaty-making between the federal government and the tribes. Settlers expected their way to be clear. You could say the word was out, the way had to be cleared for settlement.

These imposed treaties are not dead documents. They have been — and continue to be — challenged and defended many times in a century and a half.

The might and power of the United States military eight years later in the Civil War is evident by 1855, the year most Northwest tribes acknowledged federal military power and signed treaties with the United States in which they ceded large tracts of land for a portion of land reserved for them, known as reservations. The treaties also guaranteed fishing and gathering rights in places traditionally used beyond the reserved land. By the time of these treaties, Indians were already cautious about whether the U.S. government could or would carry out its promises. The treaties can be read for what they show of attitudes that have persisted in American diplomacy as well as for their central importance to the tribes in relation to the federal government ever since. The treaty with the tribe now spelled Quinault follows.

Source: Charles Kappler, *TREATY WITH THE QUINAIELT* [present spelling - Quinault], ETC., 1855.

Articles of agreement and convention made and concluded by and between Isaac I. Stevens, governor and superintendent of Indian affairs of the state of Washington, on the part of the United States, and the undersigned chiefs, headmen, and delegates of the different tribes and bands of the Qui-nai-elt and Quil-leh-ute Indians, on the part of said tribes and bands, and duly authorized thereto by them.

ARTICLE 1. The said tribes and bands hereby cede, relinquish and convey to the United States all their right, title and interest to the lands and country occupied by them, bounded and described as follows: Commencing at a point on the Pacific coast, which is the southwest corner of the lands lately ceded by the Makah tribe of Indians to the United States, and running easterly with and along the southern boundary of the said Makah tribe to the middle of the coast range of mountains; thence southerly with said range of mountains to their intersection with the dividing ridge between the Chehalis and Quinaielt Rivers; thence westerly with said ridge to the Pacific coast; thence northerly along said coast to the place of beginning.

ARTICLE 2. There shall, however, be reserved for the use and occupation of the tribes and bands aforesaid, a tract or tracts of land sufficient for their wants within the Territory of Washington, to be selected by the President of the United States, and hereafter surveyed or located and set apart for their exclusive use, and no white man shall be permitted to reside thereon without permission of the tribe and of the superintendent of Indian affairs or Indian agent....For the public convenience, roads may be run through said reservation, on compensation being made for any damage sustained thereby.

ARTICLE 3. The right of taking fish at all usual and accustomed grounds and stations is secured to said Indians in common with all citizens of the Territory, and of erecting temporary houses for the purpose of curing the same; together with the privilege of hunting, gathering roots and berries, and pasturing their horses on all open and unclaimed lands. *Provided, however,* That they shall not take shell-fish from any beds staked or cultivated by citizens; and provided, also, that they shall alter all stallions not intended for breeding, and keep up and confine the stallions themselves.

ARTICLE 4. In consideration of the above cession, the United States agree to pay to the said tribes and bands the sum of twenty-five thousand dollars....

ARTICLE 8. The said tribes and bands acknowledge their dependence on the Government of the United States, and promise to be friendly with all citizens thereof, and pledge themselves to commit no depredations on the property of such citizens....Nor will they make war on any other tribe except in self-defence, but will submit all matters of difference between them and other Indians to the Government of the United States, or its agent, for decision and abide thereby....

ARTICLE 11. The said tribes and bands agree to free all slaves now held by them, and not to purchase or acquire others hereafter.

ARTICLE 12. The said tribes and bands finally agree not to trade at Vancouver's Island or elsewhere out of the dominions of the United States, nor shall foreign Indians be permitted to reside on their reservations without consent of the superintendent or agent.

Tribal Members Speaking in the East

A Klamath headman keeps in touch with members of his tribe who are on a speaking tour in the East.

Source: Theodore Stern, *The Klamath*, Seattle: University of Washington, 1966. (From a letter dictated by Allen David to Agent L.S. Dyar and sent to Dave Hill and Tecumseh [1872], p. 276.)

I understand that you are to tell the Hias Tyee [President] how we used to live here and how we live now. After you have done this I want you to let me know how we used to live here and how we are doing now. After you have done this I want you to let me know all about it. Just what he thinks. Don't be afraid to tell us all his heart, for I'll not get afraid, nor run away. You know bad men are trying to get our lands and are lying to the President. Now if I were there I would talk the whole truth to him and would not chaco tenas tumtum [become discouraged] at whatever he might say or do. I want you to do the same. Don't be afraid of him, but tell him all about these things. Tell him that we all, both Whites and Inds,. have one Father in Heaven that we are made alike, we all have hands, feet and bodies alike, and we all have minds; In fact are brothers; and nowhere do I learn that any of us have any right to take wrongfully or by force from another any of the lands which our common Father has made for all his children.

Traditional Fishing and Its End

With the decision to build dams along the Columbia, including the Dalles Dam that wiped out the major religious, trading, and fishing site, Celilo Falls, the federal government dealt a harsh blow to Indian life that can never completely be restored. From long before the arrival of the Europeans, each year this site was an important destination for people of many tribes. In the heart of salmon-based society, it was a place where people from upriver, downriver, the coast, Puget Sound, and as far away as the Plains met for "the first salmon" ceremony, for extensive trading, and for having a good time.

The following account of dam-building, begun in the 1930s on the Columbia River, contains details told to lawyer-scholar, Charles Wilkinson by Delbert Frank of the Confederated Tribes of Warm Springs, when he recounted his family history to Wilkinson.

Source: Charles F. Wilkinson, *Crossing the Next Meridian: Land, Water and the Future of the West*, Washington, D.C.: 1992, pp. 198-199.

Word traveled fast among the fishing tribes of the basin, and they all knew about Bonneville and Grand Coulee. Feeling powerless to prevent construction of the dams or to alter their design, the Indians' main reaction was to express wonderment at why the white man would do such things. During construction, many of them came to the dam sites and watched stoically from nearby bluffs. Jim Yahtin was not there — he had passed away in 1924 at the age of 83 — but his wife, Yessessi, lived on. Her home was inland, at Simnasho, on the Warm Springs Indian Reservation, but she knew about Grand Coulee and about Bonneville, which had flooded Big Eddy. She told people about the old days and about how sad it was to flood the traditional fishing rocks. But the river still raged at Celilo Falls, and Indian people still came in from all over the basin to fish and to participate in the old ceremonies.

....

And, of course, the falls at Celilo flowed much too stoutly not to be turned into electricity. On a Sunday afternoon in April 1956, tribal people gathered on the stoop-shouldered hills to hold the "first salmon" ceremony for the last time at Celilo. Within the year Celilo Falls was gone, drowned by the pool behind The Dalles Dam. Tommy Thompson, a full-blooded Sahaptin-speaking Indian was the longtime leader of the Indians at Celilo, the person with ultimate authority to enforce all of the law ways. He cried when the water came up, saying: "There goes my life. My people will never be the same."

Restored Tribal Fishing Rights
on the Columbia River

In 1984, ten years after the Boldt decision confirmed the tribes' rights to fifty percent of the fish taken in the Columbia, The Seattle Post-Intelligencer *put out a special commemorative edition. Sportswriter John de Yonge takes a personal look back on the bitter controversy.*

Source: Charles F. Wilkinson, *ibid*. pp. 207-208.

The fish were never easy to come by for a fly fisherman like me, especially in the cold rains of winter. A good year would produce a dozen. Now when the Indian gillnets strain the river from shore to shore, my catch has become zero.

At the end of a fishless day, chilled, hungry, tired, feeling the years in my legs, my grumping has been known to have taken Judge Boldt's name in vain — sentiments which during a fishing year issue from the lips of thousands of anglers vainly stumping streams once reputed worthwhile for the excellence and abundance of their sea-run fish.

But in rational moments, I have praised Judge Boldt for accomplishing two things with his decision.

First, he was fair. To the Indians he restored a right under the law which for a hundred years had been nibbled away by the conscious and unconscious greed of people like me and by the state government's conscious and unconscious mismanagement of its fisheries wealth.

Second, and this is the good that ultimately should profit society in general, Judge Boldt's decision is forcing all of us to take a close look at how we must take care of our fisheries.

....

There is an irony that at the end of a distinguished career as a judge and as a citizen, Boldt found himself being hung in effigy and reviled for his decision on Indian treaty rights to fish.

An Armed Departure

Not everything was settled in words. Some bands ended up fighting the outsiders. Young Chief Joseph's eventual armed conflict with the American military was not unique. Neither was his punishment, which was similar to the harsh treatment handed to the Burns Paiute people, even without their taking direct part in the Bannock War. People from the small bands in the Rogue River area were also treated harshly in the aftermath of the struggles between Indians and miners.

The accounts below give perspective on The Nez Perce War — the resistance led by Young Chief Joseph in his attempt to lead his band to safety in Canada.

Young Chief Joseph and the Nez Perces

Young Chief Joseph (Nez Perce) recounts the history of his band in the first part of his well-known speech of surrender to federal military power. In the excerpt below, he summarizes the relations between his band of Nez Perces and "the men with white faces." The speech was well-known in the Indian world and beyond, appearing in 1879 in the North American Review. *Reading the whole speech will give the fullest understanding of this famous statement.*

Source: Wayne Moquin, ed., *op. cit.*, pp. 237-251.

We did not know there were other people besides the Indian until about one hundred winters ago, when some men with white faces came to our country. They brought many things with them to trade for furs and skins. They brought tobacco, which was new to us. They brought guns with flint stones on them, which frightened our women and children. Our people could not talk with these white-faced men, but they used signs which all people understand. Our people were divided in opinion about these men. Some thought they taught more bad than good. An Indian respects a brave man, but he despises a coward. He loves a straight tongue, but he hates a forked tongue. The French trappers told us some truths and some lies.

The first white men of your people who came to our country were named Lewis and Clarke. They also brought many things that our people had never seen. They talked straight, and our people gave them a great feast, as a proof that their hearts were friendly. These men were very kind. They made presents to our chiefs and our people made presents to them. We had a great many horses, of which we gave them what they needed, and they gave us guns and tobacco in return.

When my father was a young man there came to our country a white man [Rev. Mr. Spaulding] who talked spirit law. He won the affections of our people because he spoke good things to them. At first he did not say anything about white men wanting to settle on our lands. Nothing was said about that until about twenty winters ago, when a number of white people came into our country and built houses and made farms....

My father was the first to see through the schemes of the white men, and he warned his tribe to be careful about trading with them. He had suspicion of men who seemed so anxious to make money. I was a boy then, but I remember well my father's caution. He had sharper eyes than the rest of our people.

Next there came a white officer [Governor Stevens], who invited all the Nez Perces to a treaty council....Mr. Spaulding took hold of my father's arm and said, "Come and sign the treaty." My father pushed him away, and said: "Why do you ask me to sign away my country? It is your business to talk to us about spirit matters, and not to talk to us about parting with our land." Governor Stevens urged my father to sign his treaty, but he refused. "I will not sign your paper," he said; "you go where you please, so do I; you are not a child; I can think for myself. No man can think for me. I have no other home than this. I will not give it up to any man. My people would have no home. Take away your paper. I will not touch it with my hand."

My father left the council. Some of the chiefs of the other bands of the Nez Perces signed the treaty, and then Governor Stevens gave them presents of blankets. My father cautioned his people to take no presents, for "after a while," he said, "they will claim that you have accepted pay for your country. Since that time four bands of the Nez Perces have received annuities from the United States. My father was invited to many councils, and they tried hard to make him sign the treaty, but he was firm as the rock, and would not sign away his home. His refusal caused a difference among the Nez Perces.

Eight years later [1863] was the next treaty council....The United States claimed they had bought all the Nez Perces land outside of Lapwai Reservation, from Lawyer and other chiefs, but we continued to live in this land in peace until eight years ago, when white men began to come inside the bounds my father had set....The agent said he had orders, from the Great White Chief in Washington, for us to go upon the Lapwai Reservation, and that if we obeyed he would help us in many ways. "You must move to the agency," he said. I answered him: "I will not. I do not need your help; we have plenty and we are contented and happy if the white man will let us alone. The reservation is too small for so many people with all their stock. You can keep your presents; we can go to your towns and pay for all we need; we have plenty of horses and cattle to sell, and we won't have any help from you; we are free now; we can go where we please. Our fathers were born here. Here they lived, here they died, here are their graves. We will never leave them." The agent went away, and we had peace for a little while.

....

Suppose a white man should come to me and say, "Joseph, I like your horses, and I want to buy them." I say to him, "No, my horses suit me. I will not sell them." Then he goes to my neighbor and says to him: "Joseph, I have bought your horses, and you must let me have them." If we sold our land to the Government, this is the way they were bought.

There has been too much talking by men who have no right to talk. Too many misunderstandings have come up between the white men and the Indians. If the white man wants to live in peace with the Indian he can live in peace. There need be no trouble. Treat all men alike. Give them all the same law. Give them an even chance to live and grow....I have asked some of the great white chiefs where they get their authority to say to the Indian that he shall stay in one place, while he sees white men going where they please. They cannot tell me.

....

Whenever the white man treats the Indian as they treat each other, then we will have no more wars. We shall all be alike — brothers of one father and one mother, with one sky above us and one country around us, and one government for all. Then the Great Spirit who rules above will smile upon this land, and send rain to wash out the blood which is made by brothers' hands from the face of the earth. For this time the Indian race are waiting and praying. I hope that no more groans of wounded men and women will ever go to the ear of the Great Spirit Chief above, and that all people may be one people.

Recollections of a Nez Perce Woman

In 1901, a Nez Perce woman told a Bureau of Indian Affairs employee who knew her language of accompanying Young Chief Joseph and his warriors thirty years before.

Source: M. Gridley, *With One Sky Above Us: Life on an Indian Reservation at the Turn of the Century*, New York: Putnam, 1979, pp. 90-92.

My name is So-ko-mop-o and the name given to me by the white people is Jean....I am ninety years old and perhaps more....My son's name is In-mat-hia-hia and he is the only living child out of a family of nine children.

When Joseph and our people concluded to fight for his fore-father's birthright, I was anxious to join him, but my husband protested against my engaging in hostilities against the whites. Regardless of his entreaties and objections, I joined Allocott and Joseph and went all through the campaign. I left my home and my husband to assist in the struggle, caused by the encroachment of the whites. To go into details of this long and bitter fight would take much time and resurrect many unpleasant memories. During Joseph's march I often wept in sorrow and shed bitter tears in witnessing the wanton murder of so many of my relations and friends. We often hid in the underbrush and willows to screen ourselves from the musketry of the white soldiers. After such engagements the men would come and tell us who had been slain in battle. Sometimes they would bring in the mangled form of one of our braves whose life was slowly ebbing away. We always cared for the wounded as best we could until death claimed its victim. We generally buried the bodies among the rocks and in secret places. We did this so the soldiers would not know how many had been killed.

A Reporter's View of Chief Joseph

A writer for Harpers Magazine *in 1890 brought his view of Young Chief Joseph to its readers, but the article did not change the actions of the federal government.*

Source: Originally published in *Harper's Weekly*, August 16, 1890 Volume 34. (Reprinted on the Internet, http://www.indians. org/welker/joseph.htm.)

...It was probably because of business relating to the further removal of the Indians that Chief Joseph came within range of our sculptor, and found himself immortalized in clay. Though he had ridden hard for many days to reach headquarters, the old chief was fresh and alert. But, curiously enough, he found that sitting for his portrait was quite a different task from sitting a horse. Mr. Warner says that it wearied Chief Joseph exceedingly, far more than it does white men who are much less vigorous.

The sculptor says that only when some beast, bird, or insect was in sight did the old chief look the warrior and the Indian. When that was gone he relapsed into the apparently unthinking state of an animal, and showed very plainly that to remain in one position while the clay was modelling itself under the artist's fingers was a penance greater than to wait immovable for hours until game revealed itself or an enemy crept in sight.

Of this campaign General Sherman has said: "The Indians throughout displayed a courage and skill that elicited universal praise; they abstained from scalping; let captive women go free; did not commit indiscriminate murder of peaceful families, which is usual; and fought with almost scientific skill, using advance and rear guards, skirmish lines, and field fortifications." These facts only make harder the fate that awaited them, for it shows that no forbearance, no braver and generalship, are able to win for Indians justice.

A Gift to Joseph's Descendants

An aide to General Howard, C.E.S. Wood, later became an advocate for Young Chief Joseph's freedom. He also arranged for his son Erskine to live for some months in Joseph's lodge. When Erskine Wood was in his nineties, he recounted his visit for a newspaper reporter.

Source: *The Wenatchee Daily World*, June 13, 1956. (Quoted in an unpublished Memorial speech by Wood's granddaughter, law professor Mary Wood, 1997 when Wood's descendants presented the Wallowa Band of the Nez Perce with a stallion.)

Chief Joseph took me into his teepee and into his heart and treated me as a son. We ate together, hunted deer together, and slept together. I can say truthfully, knowing him was the high spot of my life.

But Erskine Wood's deep sense of gratitude and privilege also carried a deep, life-long regret:

The regret that has lived with me the longest occurred at our saying goodbye....Joseph and I sat on our horses on the Bluffs of the Columbia overlooking the river. It was time to part. My father had written me to tell Joseph that if there was anything my father could do for him he was, through me, to let my father know. I gave this message to Joseph, and he said that he would like a good stallion to improve the breed of his pony herd. I looked on Joseph as such a great man, a noble chief driven out of his ancestral home. I revered him so, that I thought his request for a stallion was too puny, was beneath him. I thought he ought to ask if my father could do anything to repair the great wrongs done him, perhaps get him back a portion of his Wallowa Valley or something like that, so that when Joseph asked for a mere stallion, I shook my head and said, "No, that was not what my father meant." Joseph accepted this calmly and we said no more. But I always regretted my utter stupidity. A fine stallion which would have upbred Joseph's herd of ponies would have been a wonderful thing for him. Just the kind of thing in his

Indian life that he needed, and of course well within the ability of my father to get for him but just because I exalted him so high I deprived him of it, and it is something I shall always regret.

From Mary Wood's presentation speech in 1997:

The [Wood] Family [now] presents the gift of a stallion in this beautiful valley in recognition of the continuing importance of the homeland to the Nez Perce people. In reaching across a century of history, The Gift carries a meaning that the bond of friendship, and a connection to a sacred place, is timeless.

A descendant of both Chief Josephs takes a political and historical stand on the Internet.

Source: http://www.indians.org/welker/joseph.htm [c. 1996].

Among the Nez Perce a great respect is attributed to the deceased and every effort is extended to insure protection of Chief Joseph's grave.

In 1928, the descendents of the Wallowa Band and Joseph's descendents got together to talk over the matter of protecting Chief Joseph's grave. It was decided that it should be moved to the edge of Wallowa Lake. When the family had exhumed the body, they had discovered Joseph's skull had been removed. They had suspected as much because of some rumored reports about it having been on display somewhere.

While I was working at the Wallowa-Whitman Nat Forest, a group of people were wanting to purchase land immediately adjacent to Old Joseph's grave site. The intent was to develop condos and such as the area next to the lake is the most prime land anywhere in northeast Oregon. Since that time, many others have joined in and want to cash in on the development.

It is certainly an understatement on my part to say that the

Wallowa is sacred to my family and descendents of the Wallowa Band Nez Perce. That land contains the spirit of our people.

Now it seems everybody wants to cash in on the Nez Perce history. When I think about it, I just get angry and I want to bite my tongue off for fear of saying bad things!

If people knew the true reasons why the whites wanted the Wallowa and pressured the government for the removal of the Nez Perce then they would understand the greed that now grips them.

Yox Kalo' (That's all)

Philip E. Minthorn, Descendent of Chief Joseph,
Cayuse/Nez Perce, Wallowa Band

Chief Joseph as an aging man on the Colville Reservation in Washington Territory, and in his younger days (Courtesy of the National Archives)

Towards "Civilization"

"Barbarous" Indian Languages, 1887

Words like "civilization" and "education" can have a double-edged meaning for Indians. Many would choose different words to describe federal boarding school policies. Following is an account by a Burns Paiute historian.

Source: The Report of the U.S. Commissioner of Indian Affairs, Washington, D.C. 1887, p. xxiiii.

To teach Indian school children in their native tongue is practically to exclude English, and to prevent them from acquiring it. This language, which is good enough for a white man and a black man, ought to be good enough for a red man. It is also believed that teaching an Indian youth in his own barbarous dialect is a positive detriment to him. The first step to be taken toward civilization, toward teaching the Indian the mischief and folly of continuing in their barbarous practices, is to teach them the English language....If we expect to infuse into the rising generation the leaven of American citizenship, we must remove the stumbling-blocks of hereditary customs and manners, and of these language is one of the most important elements.

Boarding School Days
During the Early 20th Century

Below are a Klamath's recollections of the time he spent at Yainax Boarding School on the Klamath reservation, as told to an anthropology graduate student in the early 1950s. According to the scholarly customs of the time, the man's name was not given.

Source: Hiroto, *Klamath Culture Change*, Master's thesis, Department of Anthropology, University of Oregon, 1953, pp. 248-249.

This is what we did one time — more than one time. We slipped out quietly because they'll whip us if they catch us. We ask the girls to slip us salt; sometimes they slip us bread. In the evening, we get lots of pitch, and in evening we slip out in the night, when everyone was asleep. We got spear, maybe one or two, and we light up the pitch, and we speared the fish. Maybe get five or six and take it back to boarding school, wash it out in big basin and heat water on stove, boil fish in the nighttime. We just had door light from stove, salt, and we sit around the stove, keep warm, and eat around the stove. We did this quite a bit. We never got caught. We were always lucky. The girls knew what we were doing. Four or five of us divided up the fish and eat it in the sitting room, maybe twelve o'clock at night we go to bed.

Those employees who are supposed to teach the young people were eating our food. According to the government of the United States, the government never held to the treaty they made with the Klamath Indians. You can't blame the government but the representatives. They're nothing but grafters.

....

One time me and A.M. were hooking willows from the water and a swallow came, flew up, and came close to this fellow and dropped dead. I asked, "What does this mean?" This boy said, "I know something is going to happen to me." And sure enough, his mother died one week after that. This happened when we were in boarding school when I was a tchaki. We played little while more and went home to the boarding house. I wasn't scared but I was kind of confused. He knew that something was coming to him.

Chemawa Indian School in the 1930s

Kathryn Harrison (Siletz) recalls her time at an Indian boarding school as a refuge, where she could maintain her Indian identity. This memoir was part of her statement as a member of the Siletz tribal council at the U.S. Senate hearing on S.Bill 2801 concerning the restoration of the tribe to federally-recognized status.

Source: From the hearings before the subcommittee on Indian Affairs of the Committee on Interior and Insular Affairs, 94th Congress, Second Session on S. 2801, March 30, 1976, a bill to repeal the act terminating federal supervision.

KATHRYN HARRISON: I would like to speak on Indian Identity and the struggle of maintaining that identity in the white society.

My Indianness is very important to me and has been since I was a child in Siletz. Due to the death of both of my parents at Siletz in the 1935 flu epidemic, I was eventually sent to live in a white foster home. At age 10, I was old enough to remember my parents and their way of life. Life in such a foster home was a frustrating and traumatizing experience for me. I felt rebellious at being asked to give up my Indian heritage.

As a member of a recognized tribe, I was able to attend Chemawa Indian School near Salem as an alternative to growing up in a white foster home. The happiness and satisfaction I experienced there — at age 14 — gave root to a pride in my Indian identity which I feel to this day. I can truly say those were the happiest years of my life. For once, I belonged.

A Burns Paiute Historian Recalls WWII Days

Source: Minerva Soucie, *The End of a Way of Life*, found in Carolyn Buan and Richard Lewis, *The First Oregonians*, Portland: Oregon Council for the Humanities, 1991, pp. 71, 76.

During World War II several Paiute men enlisted in the army and fought in lands they had never heard of: Germany, Africa, The Philippines, Japan, and France. Many Paiutes came back from the war highly decorated.

....

Meanwhile, Indian children at home were still not allowed into the Harney County Public Schools because, authorities reasoned, they had eye disease and were not healthy. It was not until 1948 that Indian children were allowed in the schools.

A Yakama-Cherokee Vietnam Veteran Speaks Out

Part of a longer speech by Sidney Mills, a veteran of the Vietnam War, in defense of Indian fishing rights.

Source: Wayne Moquin, ed., *op. cit.*, pp. 366-370.

I am a Yakima and Cherokee Indian, and a man. For two years and four months, I've been a soldier in the United States Army. I served in combat in Vietnam — until critically wounded. I recently made a decision and publicly declare it today — a decision of conscience, of commitment and allegiance....

I have given enough to the U.S. Army — I choose now to serve my People.

My decision is influenced by the fact that we have already buried Indian fishermen returned dead from Vietnam, while Indian fisherman live here without protection and under steady attack from the power processes of this Nation and the States of Washington and Oregon.

....

The State claims it seeks only to give equal application of law to all persons. Yet their equal application of law would permit non-Indians to catch up to 11 million salmon in all waters — yet can and does prohibit Indians from catching any in areas where the Supreme Law and their rights exist. The State claims that any other situation would give superior status to Indian "citizens," not recognizing under law that a separate and distinct status or legal dimension of the Indian exists.

....

Citizenship of the Indian has too frequently been used as a convenience of government for deprivation of rights or property held owing to our being Indians.

Near the end of his speech, Sidney Mills referred to the spending priorities of the federal government:

Interestingly, the oldest human skeletal remains ever found in the Western Hemisphere were recently uncovered on the banks of the Columbia River — the remains of Indian fishermen. What kind of government or society would spend millions of dollars to pick upon our bones, restore our ancestral life patterns, and protect our ancient remains from damage — while at the same time eating upon the flesh of our living People with power processes that hate our existence as Indians, and which would now destroy us and the way of life we now choose — and by all rights are entitled to live?

"Termination" - Free and Equal or Communities Destroyed?

During President Eisenhower's administration (1953-1956) many small and several large tribes in the Northwest were "terminated," meaning they were no longer under the supervision of the federal government and would be ineligible for federal programs. Tribal property would be divided among the members or managed by the tribal council, whichever a tribe decided. The termination policy already had supporters within the government before the Republicans gained the presidency.

How a "Terminated" Tribe Was Regarded by Other Tribes

As a Tribal Council member, testifying before a U.S. Senate Committee, Pauline Ricks spells out the importance to the Siletz of federal recognition for the tribe in its relations with other tribes.

Source: From the hearings before the Subcommittee on Indian Affairs of the Committee on Interior and Insular Affairs, 94th Congress, Second Session on S. 2801, March 30, 1976.

PAULINE RICKS: Very briefly, I would like to get across to you what restoration means to me. I speak for other people in the area that I represent as a council member. It will take a long time to heal the wounds and mend the rifts that have sapped the strength of our people. If restoration would come to us, we would once again be known as Indian people.

Our children, born after termination, would have an identity, a tribe to identify with. I cannot think of a more beautiful thing than to see our people walking tall and proud again.

Restoration would mean that we would no longer have to exist as a separate cultural group. For a terminated tribe, that is exactly what we are, even to other Indian tribes that are federally recognized. We are between two cultures. After restoration, we would again have an Indian voice in Indian affairs.

U. S. Senate Hearing on Restoration

Pauline Ricks explains that she chose to relate her grandmother's story rather than present statistics to the Senate hearing on restoring her tribe; other council members did provide statistical testimony. In 1977, the Siletz tribe became the second "terminated" tribe in the U.S. (the Menominee of Wisconsin were the first) to regain federal recognition.

Source: *ibid.*

PAULINE RICKS: But not all histories are written. To Indians, histories are passed from generation to generation by story telling. Many stories are buried deep in my heart. For I have heard the stories from my mother, who was born in 1900. She told them to me like they were told to her. So everything I have to say does not come from a history book, government documents, et cetera; nor do I quote statistics, although I have read many. It is part of my job to review Indian films, and yes, I have seen all the stereotype movies. But never have I read or seen anything like the stories I have heard from my parents. For they heard the stories from their parents, who made the long, heartbreaking journey from the Rogue River Valley up the coast to Siletz.

But one day white settlers began to move in all around them, and at first it wasn't too bad for many Indians made friends with them. They traded furs and dried foods for pretty things that the Indians had never seen before. But the early white settlers began to see the value of the rich soil. Gold was discovered and they became very greedy. Then the white soldiers came and things began to happen very fast. Ki-Ya-Na-Ha remembered how they were told to take only the clothes they had on their backs because when they got to Siletz new clothes and much food would be given them. She began to cry for she saw her people gathered up like herds of sheep. Some families were even broken up, maybe a mother in one bunch and her children in another bunch. Many fled to the mountains, for they did not want to leave their homes. But they were hunted down by the white soldiers and shot. They learned very quickly that if they wanted to live that they dared not protest.

Our trail of tears began. Ki-Ya-Na-Ha [Ms. Ricks' grandmother] was not one of the ones that rode on the ship or wagon, for she remembers walking most of the way. She told of women being abused, misused, and even kicked around by the white soldiers, especially if a mother tried to protect her young daughters. If men came to the rescue of their families, they were badly beaten and in some cases shot and left, for they were not allowed to stop and bury anyone who died along the way. She also remembered little children being kicked around if they fell too far behind.

When they got to Siletz, she told of how hungry, how tired and weary, and yes, how heartsick, for here they were on the most rugged part of the coast. Lands were not cleared. The climate was different, it was like going to a foreign country. She remembered a lot of people dying from many different kinds of diseases unknown to her, probably chicken pox, tuberculosis, she didn't know. For she always believed most of them died of depression, heartbreak and mistreatment.

State Non-Cooperation in Restoring Fishing and Hunting Rights

The Siletz tribe regained federal recognition at a price. The tribal council decided it could not overcome the "stonewalling" of the State of Oregon's Fish and Wildlife Commission and so traditional hunting and fishing rights — important both traditionally and for subsistence — were given up to gain the health and social services people needed. This letter by a U.S. Senator shows the difficult opposition faced by the tribe.

Source: *ibid.*

AMERICAN INDIAN REVIEW POLICY COMMISSION
CONGRESS OF THE UNITED STATES
Washington, D.C., March 29, 1976

HON. MARK O. HATFIELD
U.S. Senate
Russell Office Building
Washington, D.C.

DEAR SENATOR HATFIELD: The American Indian Policy Review Commission will deal specifically with the issue of Indian treaty hunting and fishing rights. At present the various task forces are pursuing their investigative responsibilities in their respective areas. In doing so the task force on Trust Responsibility and the Federal-Indian Relationship (#1) and the Task Force on Federal, State, and Tribal Jurisdiction (#4) have taken testimony from both Indian and non-Indian interests in this matter.

The reports and recommendations of the task forces will address the issues, and include an in-depth review of the relationships of different populations to the valued fish and wildlife resources. The causes for controversy and the difficult jurisdiction questions relating to Indian and non-Indian rights, will be part of this review.

We regret that Oregon Fish and Wildlife Commission failed to respond to an invitation to offer input on these important issues at joint task force hearings held in Yakima, Washington on February 2-3, 1976.

If you desire further information, please let me know.

Sincerely,
JAMES ABOUREZKH,
Chairman

Using Every Means Possible

Sarah Winnemuca Meets with President Hayes

Sarah Winnemucca, daughter of a Paiute headman, spoke for the cause of her people in lecture halls in the Eastern United States. Her words rallied Mrs. Horace Mann, wife of a leading educator, who edited her account and arranged for its publication.

Source: Sarah Winnemucca Hopkins, *Life Among the Piutes*, New York: G.P. Putnam, 1883 [reprinted 1994 by University of Nevada Press], p. 211.

"I spoke to him [President Hayes] as I had done in Washington to the Secretary and said to him, 'You are a husband and father, and you know how you would suffer to be separated from your wife and children by force, as my people still are, husbands from wives, parents from children, notwithstanding Secretary Schurz's order.' Mrs. Hayes cried all the time I was talking, and he said, 'I will see about it.' But nothing was ever done that I heard of."

Sarah Winnemucca lectured in the East about injustices to Native Americans. (Courtesy of the Nevada Historical Society)

A Discussion of Terms

A transcript from a discussion at the Oregon Legislative Commission on Indian Services.

Source: Rochelle Cashdan, *Open Our Ears: Oregon Indian Spokesmen in a State Governmental Setting*, University of Oregon, unpublished Ph.D. dissertation, 1982, pp 118-119.

Jim St. Martin (Paiute), Chairman of the Oregon Commission on Indian Services, c. 1980:

I think that part of the problem is just semantics, words. I'm not sure who started the whole process of the difference between American Indians and Native Americans.

It is my preference that people talk or refer to their own tribes or group of tribes — whichever the case may be — as point of reference and a point of identification. And I think the words American Indian and Native American are kind of catchall terms and no matter how you approach it, American Indians or whatever, I'm sure 100 years ago the Sioux and the various other tribes didn't sit and talk to themselves as being Native American, Indians or anything else, they talked about themselves being members of the tribe or a group of people....So it is my feeling that we do some contacting but also that we don't spend too much time on it.

Tribal Differences and Sameness

Speaking at a special meeting of the Oregon Commission on Indian Services on the protection of Indian burials, Esther Stutzman (Coos) explains to the archaeologists and others present that tribes share but also hold different perceptions, depending on their history.

Source: Rochelle Cashdan, *op. cit.*, pp 130-131.

Indian tribes are greatly different and greatly the same in that there are basic beliefs.

Some tribes are fortunate in that the tribes have never been assimilated —

The tribes have kept their cultures,

The tribes still have their language,

Their tradition, and their customs.

Some tribes don't.

Some tribes have been so totally assimilated that the culture is all but gone.

....

Most Indian people have very violent objections to purposeful removal of Indian graves.

It would be like an Indian tribe wanting to build a McDonald's over a white graveyard,

....

If I wanted to know more about my culture,

If all I knew is what people have known for ten years, twenty years, things like this, that'd be fine.

But if I want to know more about my culture

(mimicking) "What did they look like?" "What did they eat?" Things like that.

Because if we don't know where we've been, we don't know where we're going.

And it's probably an important part.

....

So probably what I'm doing is arguing two ways,

Don't dig them up purposely but there's also an argument for study and it depends on the individual, it depends on the tribe....

On Government Permits

Response by urban Indian Barbara Farmer (Klamath) to a government archaeologist at the Oregon Legislative Commission on Indian Services, c. 1980.

Source: Rochelle Cashdan, *op. cit.*, 1982, p. 133.

I don't think it was an Indian community was it who was officially sanctioned to dig our people up or who is, who do, have their permits?

But, I think, if they're going to continue to do that and I know there's no stopping you, at least explain it better — to the Indian people — why they have to do it. [Pause]

I mean no one ever bothers to do that.

Alaska Natives Testify to International Commission

Canadian Law Professor Thomas Berger, head of the international Alaska Native Review Commission in the 1980s, held hearings in sixty Alaskan villages (Indian, Eskimo, and Aleut) to document the views of native people about the Alaska Native Claims Settlement Act passed in 1971, which "gave" native people shares in village and regional corporations but extinguished aboriginal title to the land and aboriginal rights of fishing and hunting.

Source: Thomas Berger, *Village Journey*, New York: Hill and Wang, 1985, pp. 10, 14, 134-135.

In Fairbanks, Athabascan Sam Demientieff, the newly appointed chairman of the Doyon Regional Corporation, made this statement:

If you deal with all the problems and if you get to the point where a corporation is successful, making money, there's a lot of things that the corporation can do, and it's a tool that can be used if it is successful…[but]the corporation's not, it's not the right answer…we have to have something that reflects membership as the Native people go through generations, that they still are members of their tribe or the group that they belong to, the village.

John Smith (Tlingit) at a meeting at Metlakatla, the only reservation community in Alaska to reject the Claims Act:

We didn't want any other land. We didn't want to participate because if we did…they said, if you participate, and each one of you gets so many thousand dollars from the oil land, you'll lose the island. Everybody can come and join you. They can join you and that is it. And we — from our past experience, we know that all these years we've lived pretty well off this island. Our men don't have to beg anybody to fish any place.

A Native salmon trap in Alaska. (Courtesy of the National Archives)

Tribes Testify Regarding Remains of Kennewick Man

In the 1990s, a newspaper reported on Plateau tribes using the federal court system.

Source: Courtney Thompson and Richard Hill, *The Oregonian*, April 30, 1997, p. A14.

16 TRIBES GET VOICE ON KENNEWICK MAN

A federal judge has ruled that two Columbia Plateau tribes can have a voice in the courtroom fight over an ancient set of human remains found last summer along the Columbia River in Kennewick, Wash.

The 9,300-year-old skeleton, called Kennewick Man by scientists who want to study him and The Ancient One by tribes who want to rebury him, is the subject of an intense legal debate about a federal law intended to protect the graves and cultural and religious artifacts of Native Americans.

Scientists have sued the federal government for the right to examine the nearly complete skeleton, which they consider an invaluable link to understanding how humans first came to the Americas. They argue that the federal Native American Graves and Repatriation Act does not prohibit scientific study, which they say is needed to determine whether the ancient remains are related to any modern tribes.

American Indian tribes from the Columbia Basin consider studying the remains to be desecration. They want to rebury the remains of someone they consider an ancestor.

....

"We need to put the court and parties on notice that the tribes have an interest and that we strongly oppose the testing," said Dan Hester.

In affidavits filed in support of their motion, tribal leaders from the Nez Perce and Umatilla tribes explained why remains should be reburied quickly…."Handling human remains is an especially sensitive issue for our people," [wrote Horace Axtell, a Nez Perce Leader]. When remains are disturbed above the ground, their spirits are at unrest. To put those spirits at ease, the remains must be returned to the ground as soon as possible."

....

Alan L. Schneider, one of the Portland attorneys representing the scientists, said he doesn't think the tribes' participation adds anything new to the government's case.

"They're raising essentially the same arguments that the government is arguing," Schneider said. "We don't see our lawsuit as a claim against the Native Americans in any way. The whole case is about the government process."

The Oregon Legislative Commission on Indian Services

A reader of the following newspaper article published in 1997 would not necessarily know that Indian tribes in Oregon have been sending spokespeople to the state capitol for meetings of the Commission on Indian Services since the mid-1970s. Federally-unrecognized tribes working toward restoration were included in the meetings.

Source: "Indians Turn from Feds to States to Bolster Clout," *The Oregonian*, January 24, 1997, p. D01.

Twenty years ago, Oregon had only three federally recognized tribes, the confederated Tribes of the Warm Springs in Central Oregon, the Confederated Umatilla tribes and the Burns Paiute.

Today there are nine. Starting with the Confederated Tribes of Siletz in 1977, Congress has restored six Oregon tribes in the past two decades: the Cow Creek Band of Umpqua Indians (1982), the Confederated Tribes of Grand Ronde (1984), Confederated Tribes of the Coos, Lower Umpqua and Siuslaw (1984), The Klamath Tribe (1986) and the Coquille Indian Tribe (1989).

Most of these tribes were terminated in the 1950s in an attempt to assimilate them. Those are slowly rebuilding.

Tribal attention to state policy — whether in fish management, hunting regulations, gambling policy or educational funding financing — will continue to grow as tribes gain assets and clout.

"It will grow as tribes see that they have more resources to protect," said Karen Quigley, executive director of the Commission on Indian Services, a legislative body facilitating communication between tribes and the state. "When you have next to nothing to your name, you don't have to worry about people taking things away."

....

Louie Pitt Jr., director of governmental affairs and planning for the Warm Springs, said the tribes came together during the 1993 Legislature to strengthen laws protecting American graves and cultural items. Then the tribes got a bill introduced, which was later melded with other proposals to make tougher new protections.

Pitt said it's been difficult for governments such as his to respond quickly to the Legislature's actions. Congress moves much slower, he said, giving tribal councils time to make decisions.

Weaving the Old and the New

Skagit Storyteller - Stories as History

Vi Hilbert, a scholar-storyteller who is bilingual in her tribal language and English, translates and tells the stories of her Skagit people. Her aunt, Susie Sampson, was one of a number of Skagit storytellers who worked with scholars to record their stories in the tribal language.

Source: Vi Hilbert, ed., *Haboo: Native American stories from Puget Sound,* translated and edited by Vi Taq [superscript w] s [inverted upside-down e] blu Hilbert; foreword and introduction by Thom Hess; drawings by Ron Hilbert, Seattle: University of Washington Press, 1985. Introduction.

We do not know how long it has taken for these stories to come down to us, for we did not use the kind of calendar everyone uses today. My people marked time by referring to especially remarkable occasions, such as the year of the solar eclipse, or the period when the big log jam still blocked the Skagit river, or when the longhouses at slux (Lyman-Hamilton) still stood, or the time before the King George (British) people came. All of our culture had to be committed to memory. To this end, our historians developed excellent memories in order to pass on important information to later generations.

My aunt, Susie Sampson Peter, was a highly respected historian, who carried a heavy responsibility to pass on our culture. She and my dad were from the same family and their interest in perpetuating cultural information had been instilled by the wise teachings of their ancestors. We visited her and her husband, William Peter, often. I always stayed to listen as they ate, visited, and attended Shaker and Longhouse services.

[Aunt Susie] was a highly sophisticated raconteuse. She respected the traditional form of our stories, using the ancient beginning: Somebody lived there. She always recounted the events four times before the story came to a close. She would keep count for the audience, reminding everyone how many times this or that had happened so far in the story. She always ended in the traditional way, either dil(s)sacs or dil shuys — both mean "that's the end."

She gave a performance when she told a tale. She became the character in the story, using stylized speech for some characters. Raven always speaks with a nasal twang. She created spirit power sons for Bear, Deer, and Flounder in the story of Mink's House Party. She had interpretations for the personalities of all of her characters. She even gave voice to a dead log that was brought to life to be a babysitter for Star Child.

....

After Aunt Susie became totally blind, she lived with [her son] Martin in Tacoma. Her daughter-in-law Cecelia (Betty) told me this poignant story. Susie's bedroom was next to the kitchen and every day Cecelia could hear her telling legends to herself, while sitting alone. One day, she began a story but stopped after a few sentences, saying "Oh no, I told that one yesterday."

To the end of her days, she practiced the teachings of our culture. In order to fulfill the responsibilities of a cultural historian, she repeated her vital information every day so it would not be forgotten.

Basket-making

Nettie Jackson (Klickitat) learned basketry as an adult "when she was ready." In this Afterword to a book on Columbia River basketry, she explains the cultural, artistic, and economic meaning of her work.

Source: Mary D. Schlick, *Columbia River Basketry*, Seattle and London: University of Washington Press, 1994, pp. 199-201.

"When you want to learn something, don't always talk and ask questions, just watch and do it," my mother and grandmother told us when we were children. Even if it seems as if you can't learn, it will come to you when you are ready. I did not learn to make baskets when I was a child watching my grandmother work. I did not want to learn. It was not until 1975 that it seemed to me important I learn this part of the family tradition....I find it a lot easier for my daughter to learn because she sees me work on baskets almost every day when I am home....

There are things I do not know but am trying to learn, such as how to dye my material the natural way of my grandmothers. This is something that has changed because of the times — I use commercial dyes. I do know that my grandmother liked to try new things. My aunt had a basket that my grandmother decorated with dyed cornhusk — unusual for a cedar root basket. A bag she made had a printed bread wrapper woven in.

Every basket I make, I can sell. There are times when I want to make a basket for the sake of the idea in a certain design or for somebody I really care about. But I need money for the telephone bill, or the rent, or for fishing nets, and I hurry to finish the basket, making the traditional designs a collector will buy, so I can pay that bill.

The Indian Education Blues

Ed Edmo (Shoshone-Bannock), one of many Indian poets writing in the Northwest, combines a humorous style with serious comment in this poem.

Source: Ingrid Wendt & Primus St. John, *From Where We Speak: An Anthology of Oregon Poetry*, Corvallis: Oregon State University Press, 1993, p. 201. Also in *These Few Words of Mine*, Ed Edmo, Blue Cloud Quarterly, 1985.

Indian Education Blues

I sit in your
crowded classrooms
& learn how to read about dick
jane & spot
but

> I remember
> how to get a deer
>
> I remember
> how to do beadwork
>
> I remember
> how to fish

I remember
the stories told by the old
but

> spot keeps
> showing up
> &
>> my report card
>> is bad

Ed Edmo

Many Native languages are still in use in conversations and ceremonies. When the Kwak'wala language program was enhanced to teach primary school children how to speak it, this Alphabet Poster was drawn by Nola Johnston (1979). It was developed by the U'mista Cultural Society in Alert Bay, B. C.

"Keeping Indian"

Northwest Indians continue to live their lives as Indian people along with being American. Below you will read news reports of younger people who are keeping their Indian or tribal identities alive through performance and research.

Source: *Spilyay Tymoo*, newspaper of the Confederated Tribes of Warm Springs, July 17, 1997, p. 2.

TAILFEATHERS APPOINTED DIRECTOR OF DANCE TOUR

Local boy, Charlie Tailfeathers, Jr., was chosen to be a director of a dance troupe, "Dancers of the Seventh Feather, "traveling to Florida to perform Indian dancing June 24 to August 4. He has taken dancers from Warm Springs and Montana with him to perform various styles....Tailfeathers is seventeen years old and has danced most of his life....He will perform hoop dance, grass dance, eagle dance and play the flute. While at Riverside High School he scored high on the ASVAB test. After school he will join the Air Force for four years....

REDISCOVERED TRIBAL HISTORIES "A GIFT"
by Larry Bacon

Source: *Eugene Register-Guard*, c. September, 1997, p. 1C.

The springtime gathering on the University of Oregon campus received little publicity, but it was unprecedented in modern times.

Representatives of five Southwest Oregon Indian tribes and one from Northern California joined for the first time in 150 years for a potlatch — a traditional gift giving ceremony.

In an emotional gathering that left many in tears, they received a priceless gift from members of the Coquille Tribe. The gift? Pieces of tribal histories many had thought were lost forever.

"The information is amazing," says Amanda Siestreem, cultural coordinator for the Confederated Tribes of Coos, Lower Umpqua and Siuslaw Indians. "It's a phenomenal gift. It's going to allow us to restore a living culture."

The Coquille members offered an index of [to] more than 60,000 pages of documents mined from the anthropological archives of the Smithsonian Institution and the National Archives in Washington, D.C. A seven-member team of graduate and undergraduate students — all but one from the UO and four of them from the Coquille tribe — gathered the information during an eight-week effort in 1995.… Day after day, the team dug through boxes and scanned microfilm for anything related to the Southwest Indian tribes.

....

The director of the Smithsonian American Indian program told the Oregon researchers they had amassed more information about a group of American Indians than any previous research effort.…

Suggested Further Reading

Armstrong, Virginia I., ed. *I Have Spoken: American History through the Voices of the Indians*. Chicago: Sage Books, Swallow Press, 1971. (Gr. 5-12)

Beckham, Stephen D. *The Indians of Western Oregon*. Coos Bay, OR: Arago Books, 1977. (Gr. 5 - up).

Billard, Jules B. *The World of the American Indian*. Washington, DC: The National Geographic Society, 1977.

Bruchac, Joseph. *The Native American Sweat Lodge: History and Legends*. Freedom, CA: The Crossing Press, 1993.

Fixico, Donald. *Urban Indians*. NY: Chelsea House, 1991.

Hagen-Hammond. *Timelines of Native American History*. New York: Berkley, 1997.

Josephy, Alvin M., Jr. *The Patriot Chiefs*. New York: Viking, 1969.

Keyser, James D. *Indian Rock Art of the Columbia Plateau*. Seattle: University of Washington, 1992. (Gr. 7-12)

Lesley, Craig. *River Song*. Boston: Houghton Mifflin, 1989.

Maxwell, James A., ed. *America's Fascinating Indian Heritage*. Pleasantville: NY: Readers Digest Association, Ltd., 1978.

McNickle, D'Arcy. *Wind from an Enemy Sky*. San Francisco: Harper & Row, 1979.

Nabokov, Peter and Robert Easton. *Native American Architecture*. New York: Oxford University Press, 1989.

Rosenstiel, Annette. *Red and White: Indian Views of the White Man, 1492-1982*. New York: Universe Books, 1983.

Ruoff, Lavonne Brown. *Literatures of the American Indians*. NY: Chelsea House, 1991.

Smith, Sherry Lynn. *The View from Officers' Row: Army Perceptions of Western Indians*. Tucson: University of Arizona Press, 1990. (Grades 9-12).

Spirits of the Present (5 sound cassettes). Washington, DC and Lincoln, NE: Smithsonian Institution and Native American Broadcasting Consortium, 1995.